THE DIRT IS RED HERE

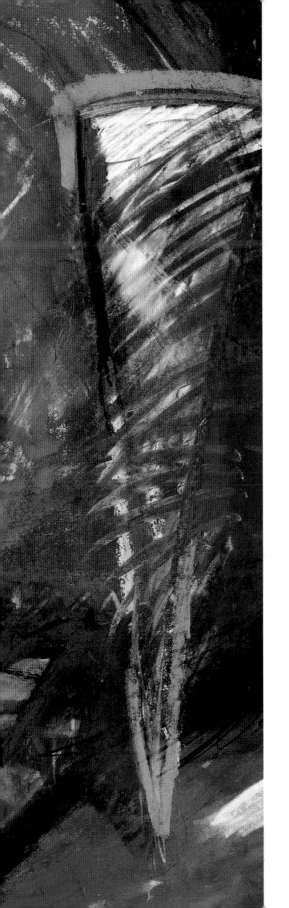

THE DIRT IS RED HERE

ART AND POETRY FROM

NATIVE CALIFORNIA

EDITED BY

MARGARET DUBIN

HEYDAY BOOKS · BERKELEY, CA

Deborah Miranda, "Baskets" and "Indian Cartography." From *Indian Cartography*, Greenfield Review Press, 1999. Reprinted with permission from the press.

Janice Gould, "Snow" and "I Learn a Lesson About Our Society." From *Earthquake Weather*, University of Arizona Press, 1996. Reprinted with permission from the press.

Janice Gould, "Doves," "To Speak Your Name," and "Three Stories from My Mother." From *Beneath My Heart*, Firebrand Books, 1990. Reprinted with permission from the press.

Wendy Rose, "Literary Luncheon: Iowa City" and "Detective Work." From *Lost Copper*, Malki Museum Press, 1980. Reprinted with permission from the press.

Wendy Rose, "Forty, Trembling," "Is it crazy to want to unravel," and "Holodeck." From *Bone Dance: New and Selected Poems, 1965–1993*, University of Arizona Press, 1994. Reprinted with permission from the press.

Library of Congress Cataloging-in-Publication Data

The dirt is red here : art and poetry from native California / edited by Margaret Dubin.
    p. cm.
Works drawn from the archives and resources of News from native California.
  ISBN 1-890771-54-6 (alk. paper)
  I. Dubin, Margaret D., 1967- II. News from native California.
  PS3537.T4753 Z6248 2002
  700'.89'970794--dc21

                                    2002004290

Title page art: Rick Bartow, *Coyote and the Dust Devil XVI*, 1993, pastel and graphite on paper, 26 x 40 inches. Photo courtesy of Froelick Gallery, Portland, Oregon.
Cover/Interior Design: Rebecca LeGates

Orders, inquiries, and correspondence should be addressed to:
    Heyday Books
    P. O. Box 9145, Berkeley, CA 94709
    (510) 549-3564, fax (510) 549-1889
    www.heydaybooks.com

Manufactured in China by Imago

10 9 8 7 6 5 4 3 2 1

CONTENTS

ACKNOWLEDGMENTS

Heartfelt thanks go out to all the poets and artists who contributed to this book. Their commitment to the arts and love for their cultures were a constant source of inspiration. I am grateful, too, for their patience and generosity to the press, and for their unflagging support of the magazine from which this book grew, *News from Native California.* I would like to acknowledge the pioneering work of Greg Sarris, who edited *The Sound of Rattles and Clappers* (University of Arizona Press, 1994), the first anthology of California Indian writers. Thanks also to Malcolm Margolin, founder and publisher of Heyday Books, whose contagious enthusiasm for all good things allowed this book to move from vision to reality, and to Frank LaPena, Shevi Berlinger, and Jeannine Gendar, who helped with everything.

INTRODUCTION

The works collected in this book sing the stories and paint the cultures of California Indians: they render the past audible and sensible to us in the present and remind us that Native California's cultural landscape is unique in the nation, diverse in its own right, and as vibrant as ever.

The poets and artists presented here hail from tribes virtually unknown to people outside California. Even within the state, few know that in precontact times more than a hundred different tribes with distinct cultures and languages flourished here. This diversity was (and still is) manifested in material culture and in masterful stories, songs, and histories passed down through the generations.

The events of colonization marginalized the histories and cultures of California tribes, leaving them largely unknown. But California Indians have not merely survived colonization, they have thrived: their numbers have grown, and they have mounted movements to revive traditional arts, relearn their languages, and gain official recognition of their sovereignty. The experience of California Indians has been so diverse and profound that the contents of this book can only start to describe it. But to make a start is important.

the contemporary
cavalry
hail stripes
& medals
but leave no trinkets
as they crush
our clamshell history
　　　　from "Independence Day," by Linda Noel

California's unique history of contact commenced with the voyages of early European explorers, among them the Spaniard Juan Rodriguez Cabrillo's three-month visit in 1542 and Francis Drake's brief landing among the Coast Miwok in 1579. Spanish colonization of Alta California began in 1769 with the establishment of missions, presidios, and pueblos along the coast from San Diego to Sonoma. Because of their locations, missions were most devastating to the coastal tribes; the Native population was reduced from approximately three hundred thousand to one hundred thousand. Northern and inland tribes escaped the brunt of Spanish colonization efforts and remained more or less intact during this first period of sustained contact. The cultural consequences of the Spanish invasion were pervasive and lasting: in the

MIKE RODRIGUEZ *Christian Kindness*, 2000, scratch-board, 17 x 11 inches. Photo courtesy of the artist.

words of L. Frank Manriquez (Tongva/Acjachmem), "The years of missionization have left contemporary Indians juggling now with then."

In 1821, Mexico won independence from Spain and acquired California. During the brief period of Mexican rule, missions were secularized and disbanded. Some Native people were allowed the use of former mission lands, but many were left to fend for themselves in an alien cash economy. In 1850, after the United States had seized California and made it a state, the federal government began to negotiate treaties with California tribes. A total of eighteen treaties were drafted, which—had they been ratified—would have established reservations of more than seven million acres throughout the state. While many tribal people supported these treaties and even abandoned lands in anticipation of their ratification, the state's immigrant landholders did not support them, mainly because they thought the treaties reserved too much of California's rich land for tribal peoples, but also because the establishment of reservations would

remove Indian labor from the settler-owned ranches. As a result, all eighteen treaties were rejected by the U.S. Senate.

In the absence of federal treaties, state military agents developed a temporary system of reservation lands to which diverse tribal peoples were forcibly relocated. Early in the twentieth century, reformers advocating for the state's many remaining homeless Indians succeeded in convincing the government to purchase plots of land to create the small group homesites that are known as rancherias. This effort was haphazard: the government has never come to terms with the unique political landscape composed of small, autonomous tribes that distinguishes Native California, and many tribes have been neglected entirely.

California tribes were dealt another blow in the 1950s, when the United States terminated its relationship with more than forty rancherias under a policy designed to force Indians into the mainstream of American culture. Since that time, several tribes have waged courtroom battles to attain or regain their federal status, but many California tribes still remain unrecognized; they have no trust land and their members do not receive the educational, housing, and medical benefits that other Native people receive. This has had a profound effect on artists, who, under the Indian Arts and Crafts Act of 1990,[1] cannot ordinarily sell their artwork as Indian-made unless they are enrolled members of recognized tribes.

After generations of being rent from their land by law and economic pressure, many tribal members find themselves living far from their aboriginal territories or communities. Some—such as Janice Gould (Konkow Maidu)—have adopted new territories, such as the multicultural urban streetscapes of Oakland and Portland; for many, however, ancestral territories have acquired additional significance as symbols of culture and markers of identity. In Deborah Miranda's (Esselen) "Indian Cartography," her father

> …opens a map of California—
> traces mountain ranges, rivers, county borders
> like family bloodlines.

The landscapes of his childhood are gone, drowned by dams and other development projects. In his dreams, he swims in the river his valley has become and

> …sees shadows
> of a people who are fluid,
> fluent in dark water, bodies
> long and glinting with sharp-edged jewelry,
> and mouths still opening, closing
> on the stories of our home.

California's tribal landscapes are diverse, ranging from the still woods and cold rivers of northern California to the burnt-gold foothills of the Sierra Nevada and the dry brush deserts of southern California. Within these landscapes, certain abiding materials—abalone, clamshell, beargrass, acorn, black walnut, elderberry—have transcended their roles in the natural environment to become signs of ethnic distinction and community membership. Bradley Marshall (Hupa) told me the story of a miniature purse he had fashioned from elk antler and presented to a friend; the friend suspended it from his truck's rearview mirror, where it identified him as Native among non-Natives, from a northern tribe among California Indians, and Hupa among the local Klamath River–area tribes.

The farther one ventures from tribal territory, the wider the boundaries of community become. When Linda Aguilar (Chumash) "signs" her baskets made of horsehair and pine needles—materials not traditional to most California tribes—with small shards of abalone or clamshell, she is proclaiming membership not just in her tribe, but in the California Indian community.

HARRY FONSECA
The Discovery of Gold in California #27, 1997, multimedia on paper, 7½ x 11¼ inches. Photo courtesy of the artist.

DUGAN AGUILAR
Two Worlds, 1998, b&w photograph,
11 x 14 inches.

Like all Native Americans, the writers and artists represented in this book live with the legacy of colonization, and this legacy emerges in their work. During the Gold Rush, a discovery that opened up the West and promised new fortunes for non-Native immigrants closed the future for many tribal people. The Native population, which had already been severely reduced during the mission period, was further reduced by at least fifty percent. Because no person alive today witnessed these events, artists rely on the powers of memory and imagination to depict them. In the summer of 1997, Harry Fonseca (Nisenan Maidu) set up his paints on the banks of the American River in order to capture the color and energy of the land and the water where John Marshall found gold in 1848. The first paintings were filled with gentle colors, the browns of the hillsides and the blues and greens of the river. As the series progressed, traces of red and gold appeared, signs of the bloodshed that resulted from the Gold Rush.

In the language of contemporary tribalism, blood has become a metaphor for Indian ethnicity. One of the most enduring legacies of colonization is that most Native Californians are "mixed-blood," the products of cross-cultural marriages or unions. Claiming this dual (or triple or quadruple) heritage is often difficult, fraught with the pain of remembered racism. Where visible differences mark inter-ethnic unions, they also point to the pain of living with the dual heritages of the colonized and the colonizer. To gain a better understanding of herself and her family, Wendy Rose (Miwok/Hopi) researched her European roots as well as her Miwok and Hopi ancestry. This didn't make their mingling in her body or her mind any easier. In an autobiographical essay for *I Tell You Now,* a collection of essays by Native American authors, she wrote: "The colonizer and the colonized meet in my blood. It is so much more complex than just white and just Indian. I will pray about this, too."[2]

Learning to claim one's tribal identity and feel comfortable with it is a process that starts early. In elementary school, Sylvia Ross (Chukchansi) told the other girls on the playground that she was part Indian, only to be scorned because the blonde (and self-proclaimed Cherokee) girl hadn't heard of the "Chik Chancy" tribe.

"That's not a tribe," she tells the girls.
They turn away laughing.
"It is," I tell them. But they don't hear.

Invisibility in the eyes of non-Indians has plagued Native Californians for decades. In the late 1950s and 1960s, the government-sponsored relocation of tens of thousands of people from other tribes to California cities made Native Californians even less visible, especially in urban communities. Janice Gould told me that when she was growing up in Berkeley, no one recognized her as Native because she didn't fit the media-generated stereotype of a headdressed Plains Indian.

Many contemporary tribal people have responded to this problem by initiating a process of personal repatriation; the return to traditions, homelands, and communities is a common theme among the artists in this book. For many, the very act of writing, painting, weaving, sewing, or sculpting creates a sense of belonging, a sense of ownership of their culture, its landscape and symbols. Richard Stewart developed a new relationship to the land of his ancestors when he saw it through the eyes of the Japanese Americans who, during World War II, had been interned at Manzanar Relocation Camp, where Stewart has worked as a tour guide for the past five years. Knowing that this site of suffering had been occupied by Paiute and Shoshone people for hundreds of years intensified Stewart's attachment to the land and his desire to understand its experience, which he pursued by writing poems inspired by traditional Japanese literary forms, particularly haiku.

Under the dark nighttime sky of weighty topics lurks a playful spirit that might be Coyote

> cruising up
> in his deluxe Ford
> eyes hidden by mirrored sunglasses,
> hooded in health club sweatshirt and
> Nikes
> unexpectedly having breakfast with
> us[3]

L. FRANK MANRIQUEZ
Coyote Paints Erotica Whilst Wearing Pajamas, 1998, acrylic, 9 x 12 inches. Photo courtesy of the artist.

or might not (this is the nature of the beast). Trickster figures are prominent in most Native North American cultures; in California, he (she?) is often manifested as Coyote. Where Coyote isn't referenced by name, his irreverent spirit is evident in stories of survival, bittersweet remembrances of childhood, and voices raised to absent gods at the random cruelty of life. Similarly, Rabbit and Mouse appear in the poems of Frank LaPena (Nomtipom Wintu), not as aging stars left over from the days of oral tradition but as the sneaky, rotten progeny of other, older animals that cannot stop reproducing. There is a certain hipness in their conversations, as there is in Harry Fonseca's early paintings of Coyote in the city. L. Frank Manriquez is particularly fond of Coyote, who functions as a kind of daring alter ego, painting erotica in his pajamas or walking toward wisdom without a map.

While familiarity with California Indian history and culture may help readers understand the works in this book by providing context, the most significant elements of any of the works are the author's personal experience and artistic preferences. Within the repertoires of the most prolific and published writers appear themes of a personal nature: Janice Gould writes about rejection, love, and sexuality; Wendy Rose writes of abuse endured throughout childhood, abandonment, and discrimination within her chosen field of academia. In an autobiographical essay, Rose confessed that everything she has "ever written is fundamentally autobiographical, no matter what the topic or style."[4] Rose needed poetry, in fact, to exorcise the painful events of her childhood, because plain, narrative text failed her. "If I could look my childhood in the eye and describe it," she wrote, "I would not have needed to veil those memories in metaphor."[5]

Much of the art presented in this book is, indeed, as autobiographical as it is tribal. This does not mean it is nostalgic or inaccessible. Quite the opposite: the depth of human emotions echoes the power of remembered histories to make each of these works meaningful and accessible to every reader. Taken together, as a body, the works transcend each and every medium (words, paint, grass, shell) to convey something enduring about the California Indian experience and true about humanity.

1. The 1990 law amended an earlier law, the Indian Arts and Crafts Board Act of 1935, to give the Indian Arts and Crafts Board more power. The new law also increased the penalties for fraudulent representation.
2. Brian Swann and Arnold Krupat (editors), *I Tell You Now: Autobiographical Essays by Native American Writers* (Lincoln: University of Nebraska Press, 1987).
3. Excerpt from *Where You First Saw the Eyes of Coyote,* by Linda Noel (Strawberry Press, New York, 1983).
4. From Rose's essay in *I Tell You Now.*
5. Ibid.

THE DIRT IS RED HERE

SNOW

JANICE GOULD

Snow had fallen during the night,
snow on snow. The streets were white and muffled,
and hard banks had piled up along the sidewalks,
on the boulevard where city buses chuffed to a stop.
It seemed we disembarked into caves of ice,
into dirty passages broken through by passersby
heading for home after the five o'clock
rush from downtown.

I liked the snow, the way the city slowed
to accommodate Nature
who slid her hand over the northwest,
from Puget Sound
to the Willamette Valley,
from Tillamook to Hood River,
until fields, forests,
the rounded hills and orchards
all lay in a deep frosty dream:
ponds frozen over,
cattails split like cornhusks.
Horses in pastures,
breath steaming, icicles
hanging from their shaggy coats.

The morning after the snow
it was just growing light.
And probably for the first time
I saw two adults in love.
He had walked out from their basement apartment,
laughing as he pushed through
that trench of cold powder,
a stocky black man

in a bus driver's uniform.
She was at the door, laughing with him,
her blond hair disheveled,
her face puffy.
She smoked a cigarette, he held
a cup of coffee.
Before quite reaching the street
he had to come back to kiss her.

That is what I saw
as I watched from my window:
him waving to her from the corner
he strode through the snow,
the fresh swirl blown down like feathers
or cottony seeds.
                            That winter, for me,
was a time of transition.
Yet everything seemed to fit together:
how you and I read Cesar Vallejo,
drank strong French coffee,
and ate chunks of bittersweet chocolate.
How the soft sounds of Portuguese
fit in my mouth
as we studied from one of your books.
How every day, downtown, we passed
the family of women who stood
in a storefront window
at the foot of Burnside Bridge—
women young and old,
their faces hardened,
black hair pulled tight
against their thin heads.

2

I believed they were gypsies
who could see into my soul.

They would have seen how I
was in love with you,
a girl who was a little crazy,
who had hung her heart
in the icy branches of a tree
beyond the reach of
father, mother, or lover.
How stupidly I behaved with you.
But I was young, frightened,
and also crazy.
I didn't know the dimensions
of abuse and violence;
I was still unnerved
by the word "lesbian,"
how it began with a shameful lateral,
how the sibilance of its interior
fit against the body with its wetness,
its caverns,
its long dream of winter.

Perhaps that's why I like
to think of the busman and his woman,
the warmth that flooded out their door
as if they'd stepped from their hot sheets
to the shower, to the breakfast table
with its cups of coffee,
how their flesh was still flushed
with blood and kisses.

                    I know this now,
the depth of roses, the laughter
that resounds in frozen air,
the first shove though January snowfall.
After years I grew up,
married a woman who isn't crazy.
I like to imagine how
I've come back to kiss her,
time after time on snowy mornings,
her lips warm,
the room steaming,
the smell of sex still in our bed
delicious as sweet rolls and tangerines.

I LEARN A LESSON ABOUT OUR SOCIETY

JANICE GOULD

Late November on our way to work
you pulled the cord and the bus stopped
this side of the Alameda tube.
"I've got to get out of here,"
you told me abruptly.
"Please, don't follow me."
I looked in your face
but you wouldn't look back.
You were nervous,
your eyes moving everywhere.
"I'll phone," you said.
I watched you push your way
through the press of students,
secretaries, the eight a.m.
crowd on their way to work.
Eyes glazed, you stepped off the bus.

I didn't know then it was epilepsy
that jerked you to your feet,
and like a pistol against the skull,
compelled you to walk,
walk, making your way to 14th Avenue,
your jaw clamped as if it had been wired closed.
You know places where you could abort the attack
with heroin: back porches
where men of every color shot up,

a hard gang of hard-asses, and you,
skinny and tough as the boy
you wished you could be.

Those were times of no time for you,
weeklong blackouts in which you lost
all trace of your history,
name, or family.
Your kids would be alone in the house,
eating cold hot dogs and white bread.
They were used to taking care of themselves.

After an attack, you woke here or there
and had to find your way home.
Sometimes you came to on the stone
cold floor of a cell.
Other times, like that day,
you ended up in the hospital
on some ward in the basement,
strapped down on a table.
The nurses and orderlies abused you,
kept the restraints on you for hours.
They despised you for being an addict,
a queer, at the mercy
of an illness.

LORENCITA CARPENTER *Fall to Earth,* 1997, b&w photograph, 8 x 10 inches.

DOVES

JANICE GOULD

Our lives go on viscerally, austere, beneath our memories. You are the girl with bruised knees, her summer dress spattered with blood, grief, shame, and a man's sperm, something torn as he pushes you down on the heap of clean laundry you carried home that evening, walking barefoot on the street. I am the child who examines the body of a mourning dove in its shoebox, feathers colored ivory and blue beneath pale brown. Kneeling in the woods where moss and tall grasses grow, we know how to pray, how to have a funeral. I don't want to go there alone, or to the shed where, in the dark, bicycles are stored, and old rope.

LORENCITA CARPENTER *Reborn,* 1997, b&w photograph, 8 x 10 inches.

THREE STORIES FROM MY MOTHER

JANICE GOULD

Prayer Path
We stand beneath the buckeye tree,
and the big pods rattle in the wind.
Blind grandma listens and sometimes sings
in a voice already like a ghost's.
Her hand rests on my shoulder:

I am her eyes.
I shift my weight and strain to hear
the voices she attends.

Grandma has staked the other world to our own.
The day she leaves, no longer blind,

she will follow a trail of feathers,
tassels hung to elderberry,
knots of long, bent grass.
She will walk quickly
like a young thing
down the dim trail.

Cure Night
Mama became very sick
when something puffed in her side
like a boil.
Her limbs were soft-boned,
her eyes pockets of pain.
Finally she had no voice
to call us from play,
so she lay down
and began to wait for death.
Papa rode out of the canyon
and brought the medicine man from Humbug
    Valley.

The old man chanted that night,
shaking the deerskin rattle.
He blew smoke across mama
and sucked at her sore side,
trying to draw between his teeth
what remained swollen in her.

Late in the night he stopped singing,
and in the silence
we heard the crackle of fire,
the hiss as lamps burned low.

Wind dragged itself down the creek
and seeped into the rafters of our house.
Words came in a strange high language.

The old man sighed and turned to my father,
saying no Indian medicine could change
the day of her last breath.

She Comes Home
Dad took mama up to Quincy.
White doctors removed the tumor.
Maybe because she was a half-breed
they were careless how they sewed her up.
They sent her home on the train.

Her life slipped away
as the Southern Pacific snaked down the canyon.
Its brakes groaned on the long grades,
and a hemorrhage appeared on the folds
of mama's cotton dress.
There was heat glare
on mica and serpentine.

Perhaps she watched the river,
the way it bucks and eddies
and swirls in the deep pools.
Perhaps she took in the deep blue of the sky,
noticed wind catching in the aspen,
saw patches of snow saddling the razor-back ridges.
It was thirty miles of pain
to where we kids were waiting.

At Belden station
the men strapped her to a chair
and carried her into town.
Already she was moaning
in a voice so changed and low
it belonged to no woman.

In that sound she drifted,
unaware it was death who sang.

CANNERY, HOOD RIVER

JANICE GOULD

In September the pears were trucked in
from the orchards and dumped into bins
that crested with ripening fruit.

We stood for hours by our machines
as the harvest jostled by on conveyors, timed
our movements to the rhythm of the steel
peelers. We fed the cups that grabbed the fruit
—six pears at a time—clamped them tight,
skinned, slit, and sent them to the next

group of women who sorted the halves
from the bits and quarters, trimmed the pieces
of excess hide. When the noon whistle blew,
we broke for lunch in the company cafeteria,

sat at the square tables, downed our chili,
joked and complained about men, work, our pitiful
pay, for which we were grateful nonetheless.
On days it didn't rain, my friends and I escaped

to the grassy slope near the county library,
ate apples, dozed in the Indian Summer sun.
I could hear the tugs on the Columbia pushing
their freight of logs or grain, and sometimes

a sailboat slipped past, tacking down the river
to the Pacific. I could feel the pull of a current
in my own blood, and curiosity welled in me
about what lay beyond where I could see. When

we heard the blast of the signal at one, we'd return
to work, don our aprons, make haste to our peelers
at the back brick wall. Above the din of the factory,
clank of cans, and whir of machines, we stood

guarding our unfulfilled dreams.

RICK BARTOW *Nickwitch*, 1994,
pastel and graphite on paper, 50½ x 48 inches.
Photo courtesy of Froelick Gallery, Portland, Oregon.

RICK BARTOW
Above: *Fox Spirit,* 2000, mixed media sculpture, 20 x 25 x 9 inches. Left: *Questions of Beliefs,* 1993, pastel and graphite on paper, 40 x 26¼ inches. Photos by David Browne, courtesy of Froelick Gallery, Portland, Oregon.

BUTTERFLY

DARRYL WILSON

STOP!! Stop the car! Hurry! Slow down!

"I'M TRYING TO! What am I stopping for?"

"Jest stop!"

Sometimes she amended her "just" to "jest," particularly when she was excited.

I worked the car off the road, dust swirling behind. Before the car came to a full stop, sputtered, then died, she was out running to the front. She worked something loose from the hood, put it in her palm and, looking into her hand, carefully, she got back in with me. Cupping one hand over the other, she let me "peek." Like a wrapper for a queen, a little, golden-yellow butterfly lay there, wings tightly closed. A little leg moved so it was alive, damaged but alive.

Like she would do with her twin babies later on, she made up a song, something she could hum. She hummed, saying "mothie is here" several times.

We continued on down the road to the swimming hole. "Love, look!" she shrieked. In a cloud of dust, I stopped the car, the familiar sputter, it died again. There on the flat of her palm, standing tall and exercising its wings, her butterfly. She watched its every movement and her tender countenance was as though she just gave birth, or gave life—much more than sacred, preciousness wrapped around wonder, breathtaking.

When we reached the swimming hole—which was about hip deep, but with clear hurrying water and instead of gravel on the bottom, it was coated with agates of many colors nearly all worn smooth and round (her favorite, red)—her butterfly flitted away. She watched it, expecting it to be going to a happy place, and she was happy for that.

The next day she was cleaning house. The door was open. I could hear the "swish" of her broom. Sunday. My morning walk took me by a little pond. Looking for nothing in particular, I spied through the thicket embracing the water hole a branch with a cocoon expertly attached to it and hidden from most hungry varmints. Wanting to take her a present, I thought she might like it, so broke the branch, not disturbing the sleeping larvae, and took it home with me.

"Don't leave that stick laying around. I am cleaning house!"

"Okay, but it is not just a stick, it's your baby."

I turned the branch slightly and she examined the cocoon, noticing how it was fastened. "What is it? What do I do with it?"

Keep it warm and safe. Sing to it. Worry about its future. Think about it. Just like a baby.

"When do I start?"

"Maybe you already started."

So for the next few weeks she wondered what it was, hummed the little song, worried a little, and planned for its future—whatever that might be.

"Love! Love! LOVE!"

She was in the house screaming at me through the kitchen window. I thought maybe she cut herself or something. I rushed in. There resting in her hand, her "baby." A black and orange butterfly.

She was flushed reddish-gold and her eyes (squinted, still all the world reflected silver there) were filled with some kind of disbelief mixed with a great accomplishment. She was holding her breath. Isolated strands of her hair caught the sunshine, magically creating a halo of fine copper. Then she breathed. I would see that sweet, human landscape again—when she held the twins for the first time.

LORENCITA CARPENTER
Fresh, 1997, color photograph, 4 x 6 inches.

JEAN LAMARR Above: *Going Back to the Rez,* 1974, acrylic on canvas, 48 x 36 inches. Right: *Chains for Freedom,* 1993, mixed media on canvas and handmade paper, 24 x 36 inches. Photos courtesy of the artist.

MAYBE THEY COULDN'T MAKE THE SHOE FIT THE FOOT

LINDA NOEL

For Clara and those who waited

Bring some shoes to the rancheria. They never did.
No,
All the people waited though.

His gramma remembered
They all washed their feet that day.
The man was coming all the way from Sacramento.

They waited and waited.

Finally he came, but he didn't bring no shoes.
He took some paper and measured their feet,
Got their sizes and said he would bring shoes back.

And all the Indian people were glad 'cause they
    didn't
Have no shoes.

They waited and waited.

He never did return.

Phil's gramma would laugh remembering the story
Of the whiteman bending at the feet of old Indian
    women
Who had never before worn whiteman shoes.

They wondered what he thought.

There was something about how he would measure
    the foot,
Then write it down and look at them as if to say
What odd and ugly feet.

The old women's laughter is our own as we speak:

> Maybe they didn't know how
> To make shoes to fit Indian feet,
> Or maybe the sight of their feet
> Frightened him away.

GEORGE BLAKE
Dude Boot, 1995, elk antler, silver, and black leather,
8½ x 11½. Photo courtesy of the artist.

LESSON IN FIRE

LINDA NOEL

My father built a good fire
He taught me to tend the fire
How to make it stand
So it could breathe
And how the flames create
Coals that turn into faces
Or eyes
Of fish swimming
Out of flames
Into gray
Rivers of ash

And how the eyes
And faces look out
At us
Burn up for us
To heat the air
That we breathe
And so into us
We swallow
All the shapes
Created in a well-tended fire

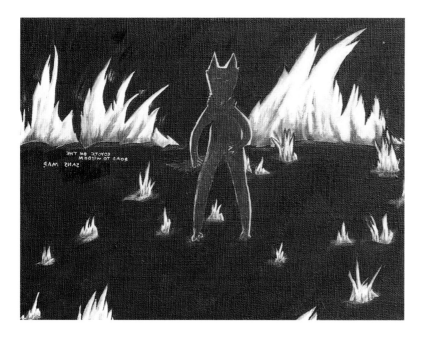

L. FRANK

Coyote on the Road to Wisdom Sans Map, 1997, acrylic, 9 x 12 inches. Photo courtesy of the artist.

L. FRANK

Acorn Boy, 1998,
acrylic on raw can-
vas, 9 x 12 inches.
Photo courtesy of
the artist.

INDEPENDENCE DAY

LINDA NOEL

real cowboys
& fake indians
walk the hot asphalt
of downtown america
gravel & tar
pave the patriotic
path
of rodeo queen
& faceless brass
march to the beat
bellowing
national pride
the contemporary
cavalry
hail stripes
& medals
but leave no trinkets
as they crush
our clamshell history
with every step

justice parades
main street
in waxed convertibles
& pioneer families
on horseback
tilted stetson
shades
sun glasses
sun burn
& spurs
mark the face
of america
red white & blue
flags
fly high
through staggered
heat waves
and fireworks
false star designs

BRADLEY MARSHALL

Abalone Necklace (detail), 1998, abalone, beargrass, piñon nuts, metal coins, glass beads. Photo by Father Vogel Marcel.

RAIN BELIEF

LINDA NOEL

swollen
sky
sing us some rain   sway
oak arms   shed
your blue clothing   let
free your moist flesh   flung
against bone windows   flaunt
your sleek body   fly
above thirsty dreams   fall
into my parched canyon throat   fill
my river up   fool
me into thinking wetness is enough   watch
me flood myself   feed
the memory
                              melt mountains
                                                  make mud

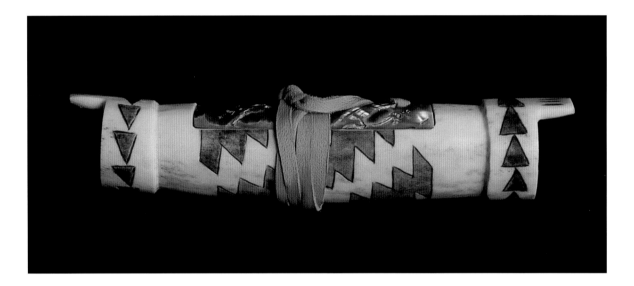

BRADLEY MARSHALL
Above: *Elkhorn Purse*, 2000, elk antler, deerhide,
abalone. Right: *Girl's Ceremonial Dress* (details), 2000,
deerhide, abalone, glass beads, beargrass, piñon nuts.
Photos by Father Vogel Marcel.

I FLEW WHEN I WAS YOUNG

FRANK LAPENA

Long ago
when I was
young and small

My mother
who believed
in holy things

took me
to visit a
blessed person

where I repeated
sacred words
of prayer

when we went
outside I rose
toward the sun

with lightness
and a feeling of joy
I left the ground

Now as I think back
I wonder about
that prayer
the sun and flying

And the truth
and power
of those words

JAMES LUNA
Ascension (details), 1998, performance/installation.
Photos courtesy of the artist.

RABBIT CRAZY

Rabbit laughed and slapped his knees
Oh lord you're really something
and mouse laughed back

They were talking how rabbit
got so many girls and what it takes
to keep them happy

It must be something real good, "Yeah
for a ninety year old…" he's saying
but he's really 62
which ain't bad for a rabbit

"They are from 18 to old…"
He's talking of his women
I wonder who "they" are
and what he means by "old"

One time, rabbit to show
his friendship offered to
let mouse use his name
for one of rabbit's children

Mouse's wife said
she would beat him
if that happened
and mouse and rabbit laughed

They laughed as they talked
of women and babies
and what it takes to be
a crazy rabbit or a lover man

THE UNIVERSE SINGS

Spring days
and winter nights
have beautiful
flowers shining
they make themselves
visible
by whispering
in the color
of blue pollen

Their fragrances
are footprints
lightly traveling
on the milky way

Once I was given
a bracelet of
golden yellow flowers
on velvet darkness

Reenie said that
a mouse was painted
in the color of the sun
and that he danced for joy
on seeing flowers
blossom into stars
dancing across the universe
and singing,
singing, singing.

WE LAUGHED AT MEMORIES

I wanted to stretch my imagination
to the sounds
of "old times"
when we were young

I will see you later
I told him
which meant anywhere
from a week to whenever

But the phone call forced me back
and emphasized the
obligatory nature of promises

It's like that saying, "see you
next week" and the person dies
with his secret intact
and sealed with honey,
and bears and bees
singing and humming
the feast of life

We used to laugh
about our mutual friends
and common disabilities
like old age and falling
down hills and having young
women and not being able
to do anything about it
but God knows we tried

I see the humor
and laugh out loud
at the memory
of blue cataracted eyes
that forced him and now us
to eat air
and the same piece of meat
three times

Our stories are like that
with interruptions and
story lines missing
by the space of seconds,
hours, days and months

My friend reminds me
of that. I can almost
hear his brain turning over
The best kept secret
is the most common thing
in the world; we laugh.
We laugh at memories.

(Sacramento, 2001)

JUDITH LOWRY

The Obedient Wives, 2001, acrylic on canvas, 65 x 90 inches.
Photo by Rob Wilke.

A BURIAL BURN

FRANK LAPENA

We have come to
sing you away
with acorn meal
wormwood and bearhide
And the song

We have come to
put the world's things aside
with the lowering of
the box and the song

We have come to
cry this last time
and two of us dance
for you while the women sorrow

We have come to
dance for you
and each step is
done over the box
leaving footprints
in the dirt

We have come to
burn you away
and funeral poles
remind us of you
And I am crying

We have come
to sing you away
but the only sounds
are tears dropping
slowly in our mourning

We have come to
remember what it
is to die a good death
and what it is to live

We have come to say
goodbye with embers
smoke and ashes in the
grey of morning

JUDITH LOWRY

The Rescue, 1999, acrylic on
canvas, 68 x 80 inches.
Photo by Rob Wilke.

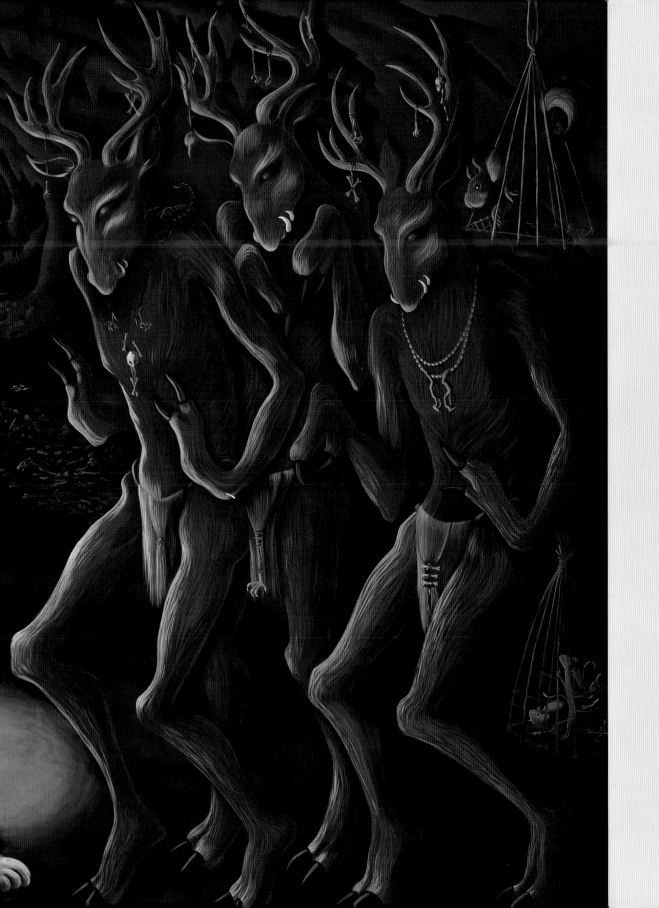

INDIAN CARTOGRAPHY

DEBORAH MIRANDA

My father opens a map of California—
traces mountain ranges, rivers, county borders
like family bloodlines. Tuolomne,
Salinas, Los Angeles, Paso Robles,
Ventura, Santa Barbara, Saticoy,
Tehachapi. Places he was happy,
or where tragedy greeted him
like an old unpleasant relative.
A small blue spot marks
Lake Cachuma, created when they
dammed the Santa Ynez, flooded
a valley, divided
my father's boyhood: days
he learned to swim the hard way,
and days he walked across the silver scales,
swollen bellies of salmon coming back
to a river that wasn't there.
The government paid those Indians to move
   away,
he says; I don't know where they went.

In my father's dreams
after the solace of a six-pack,
he follows a longing, a deepness.
When he comes to the valley
drowned by a displaced river
he swims out, floats on his face
with eyes open, looks down into lands not
   drawn
on any map. Maybe he sees shadows
of a people who are fluid,
fluent in dark water, bodies
long and glinting with sharp-edged jewelry,
and mouths still opening, closing
on the stories of our home.

PETROGLYPH

Snow falls that night,
spreads heavy and smooth
like stone, like white granite.
It takes the sharp cut of deer tracks.

In nightgown and bare feet
she follows them, a string
of cloven hearts wandering up from the woods,
past the barn with its scents of straw,

cats, cobwebs; lapping the length
of the skinny tin trailer
where the girl had lain curled
in dreams of slow words; past

her father's red truck
asleep in the driveway, dents filled with snow,
tools covered in the bed made
fresh and clean, no traces

of labor, his sweat, jumbled scraps of lumber; down
the long driveway, to enter
mute pines and bare maples
at the mouth of the road that leads away.

She stands breathing in silvered swirls, heart
thumping; this is as far as I go. Snow
takes her print, curved half-moons
cut by the heat of childhood in her skin.

DEER

They hang her in the barn, head down, tongue fat,
dripping blood. I am left alone
for a moment, venture close to stroke dark fur
made rough by winter; that is when she is still
whole, intact, before butchering. I'm not sure
if they shot her or hit her by accident
with the truck, but she comes from the mountains
out of season so it is the darkness that counts, not
how she died. All winter long we'll eat her
in secret: steaks, stews, bones boiled for broth
and the dogs. But what I will remember are men's
    hands—
fingers stained with oil and blood—
the rough way they turn back the hide, jerk down hard
to tear it off her body. A dull hunting
knife cracks and disjoints the carcass.
Dismembers it piece by piece.
The hide disappears—left untanned, buried,
taken to the dump. For years afterward
I walk out to the barn, scrape my foot against
the stained floor beneath the crossbeam, never tell
    anyone
                I've been taken like that:
without thanks, without a prayer, by hands
that didn't touch me the way a gift should be
    touched,
knives that slid beneath my skin out of season
and found only flesh, only blood.

THE LANGUAGE OF PROPHETS

Out of grey clouds
right to left
one hawk
eight herons
over dark water.
One fierce year—
eight years of stillness.
Green pines take
what fog lets go.

BASKETS

DEBORAH MIRANDA

*"The Museum's collection…inspired this Chihuly
series of glass work."*
—Washington State Historical Museum exhibit

When Chihuly saw you, he thought
curve, slump, weight.
He felt the smooth sweep
of glass blown into gravity.
When I see you, I open
from an empty round place
dark as stems of maidenhair fern

or the fingers of women
who twined your strength
with reeds and tule, grass and cedar bark.

Labels gleam clean as catalogued prayers.
Twana Skokomish #157 stretches
with a belly-shaped need to hold.
Klickitat #105 rises to receive
camas root and blackberries.
Yakima Sally #24 unfolds toward water,
salmon stitched with purpose.

LINDA AGUILAR

Above, from left: *Jingles, Bells, Shells, and Polliwogs,* 1999, black horsehair, abalone, shells, metal bells, and waxed linen thread, 12 inches wide; *Whirlwind Basket,* 1998, black horsehair, waxed linen thread, porcupine hair, and turquoise, 6 x 3 inches; *Flower,* 1998, brown horsehair, waxed linen thread, and seed beads, 5½ x 2 inches. Opposite, left to right: *Untitled,* 1998, white horsehair, waxed linen thread, buffalo wool, 3½ x 1½ inches; *Tools,* 1998, dyed buffalo bone, bone and horn beads, and glass beads, 6 x 3 inches. All photos by Tim Browne.

Indians evolve like everyone else.
I understand safety pins on regalia,
plastic pony beads,
synthetic sinew.
Times change. We grow into
what comes next.

But when I see you, baskets—
locked in cabinets,
behind glass,
preserved in shadows—

I tear wide with want
for the press of my palm
against rushes, willow, redbud;
for beargrass lips frayed and soft
against my cheek. At the edge of the room
old mouths whisper weave, braid, fill.
I take the coiled voices of women
into the walls of this hollow vessel.

POEMS BY RICHARD STEWART

"DOG POLICY"

The reservation,

    a cage for my soul?

NO!

I am not a dog.

I am a bird,

    a slight movement in the air.

*This is for Harold H. Morimizu, who was held
prisoner at Heart Mountain in Wyoming.*

"B" STREET

One day, walking on "B" Street,
I thought of drinking sake,
eating rice,
medaka,
Little Tokyo,
Boyle Heights.

Hideo said,
"You are an old Japanese
come back
as a Paiute Indian."

We drank and talked
    far into the past.

BRIAN TRIPP
You Should Know My Place, 1987, mixed media sculpture,
46 x 12 inches. Photo courtesy of Frank LaPena.

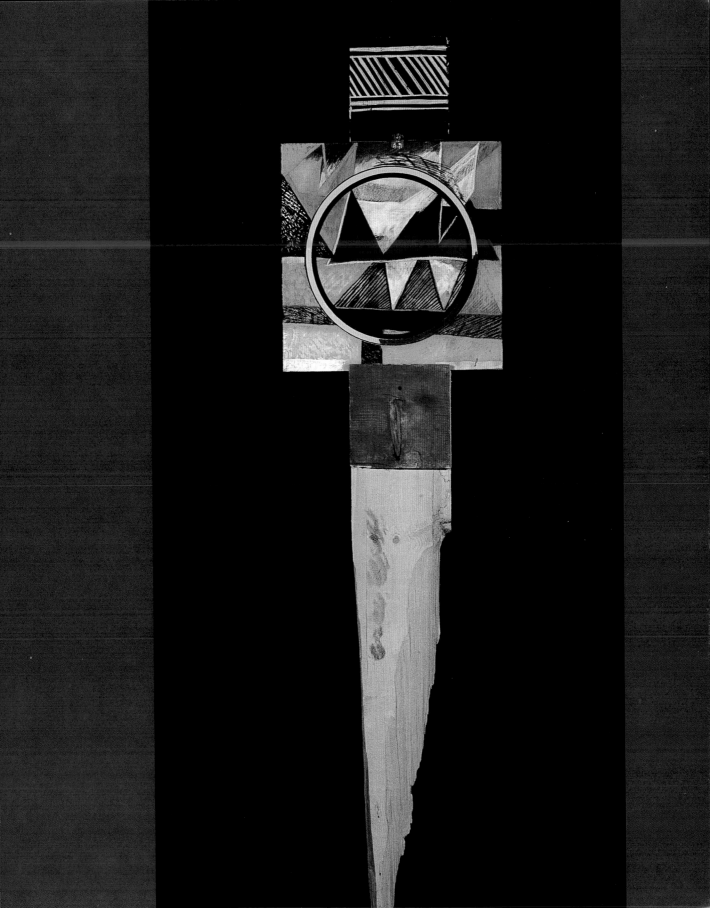

PEAR ORCHARD

I carry no tape recorder,
no pen or notebook.

I talk,
listen,
talk,
listen,

in endless round.

The crows
have eaten
most of the pears.

KAMI

Peering over clump
of wild rose bushes,
a young coyote
watched me,
as I listened to the wind
spilling

through the tree leaves.

HARRY FONSECA
Rose and the Res Sisters, 1981, lithograph, 30 x 22 inches.
Photo courtesy of the artist.

Creation 2001, 2000, multimedia on canvas,
6 feet, 1 inch x 17 feet, 3 inches. Photo courtesy of the artist.

PILGRIMAGE

...pottery shards,
 cobalt blue,
fragments of history
        scattered
        on the decomposing ground.

An occasional marble,
the odd button;
I pass "go" pieces several times,
but don't collect $200.00.

Isolation
 is the most profound aspect
        of Manzanar.

NO-THOUGHT

...near the old bamboo,

there is one stone
    that fits my backside

        just so.

DUGAN AGUILAR
Harry Fonseca, 1998, b&w photograph, 11 x 14 inches.

TRIBAL IDENTITY GRADE THREE

SYLVIA ROSS

The recess bell rings and we rush
for the hopscotch game
before the fourth grade is out.

Sister talked about the Plains Indians.
We saw a film on Navajos.
We colored a ditto of a pueblo.

Lisa brags, "I'm part Indian.
I'm Cherokee." She flips her blonde
curls and her feet own the ground.

"Me too," I say. "I'm part Indian too."
"Well, what are you then?" she says.
"I'm Chik Chancy," I answer.

"That's not a tribe," she tells the girls.
They turn away laughing.
"It is," I tell them. But they don't hear.

I take out my hair clip
to use as a lagger in the game
and dark wisps fall over my face.

The clip hits the sixth square
and then ricochets out past the line.
I pick it up and put it back.

Chik Chancy is a tribe.

FRITZ SCHOLDER
Indian Kitsch (details), 1979, photocollage.
Photo by Bill McLemore.

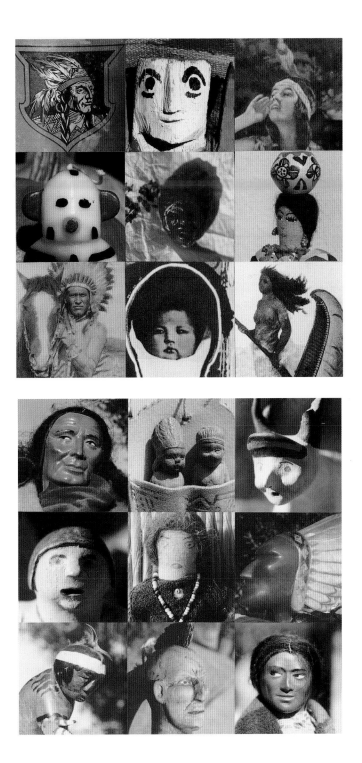

47

POEMS BY SYLVIA ROSS

SISTERS

Talking at the table until late
When everyone else is asleep

Sister, we are the bear women
We wear abalone shell necklaces
We carry baskets
We hold our men in great bear women
Arms

Sister, we were too far apart
In our births
We never played together
Never danced with
the same boys
Didn't share small children
Like other sisters did

But while you talk
Our mother's voice comes out of
Your wonderful bear woman mouth
Our mother's laugh shakes your belly
Though it is much smaller
Than hers ever was

My sister, we are the bear women
We have the power
To crash through brush, to smash
The clouds and pluck stars down
To make a meal

Sister, tonight your voice
Brings our mother back to us
Her great bear woman presence
Fills all the space
Of this room.

IN THE HILLWIFE'S KITCHEN

It wasn't so much
that she minded rowdiness
the grab-ass revelry
the plate breaking
milk spilling
loud and careless
counter bashing
rambunctiousness
that came when they all
happened to be home
at the same time

or that she preferred
the empty sink quiet
of so much of the rest
of her year
but the draggy solitude
filled days
orderly and scrubbed
stretched out her time
like hands pulling
at taffy or
kneading dough

and this homecoming
crowded her
with great rib crushing hugs
iron skillet wit
laughing profanities
apron snagging humor
and endless cooking
it reminded her
how some meals
hard to prepare
can be too quickly eaten

MATRILINEAL
DESCENT

The only picture I have
Of my great-grandmother
Shows her lying
In her coffin.
No one thought to take
A picture of the Chukchansi
Woman
Until time had passed away.

The best picture I have
Of my grandmother
Shows her holding
Her sister's stillborn boy.
He was a fat and beautiful baby;
She looks down at him.
Seems like no one
In my family
Thinks about time
Until it is gone.

I have lots and lots
Of pictures of my mother.
But none show her
Standing in the kitchen
Apron stretched
Across her fat belly
Dimples winking
From her round cheeks
As she tells some truth
Funnier than lies.

Seems like time is a mean
Woman,
Too beautiful, and too proud,
To let any ordinary people
See her.

COWBOYS AND
INDIANS

My mom said her grandmother
Loved the cowboy's blue eyes
And he loved her low voice
And shy ways
And he'd never known
A woman who could skin
A rabbit so fast.

Then her mother in turn
Found another cowboy
With blue eyes.

So we ended up pale.
One of my brothers even has
Blue cowboy eyes.

I'm a dark-haired woman
With a low voice
And shy ways
Like all those women
Before me.

I don't know if I could skin
A rabbit so fast.
I don't even know if
I could skin a rabbit.

I think I could.

BLACKBERRY WINE

SHAUNNA OTEKA MCCOVEY

Grandma slammed the bottle
down on the table, and
it burst
into a wind of
green shards
caught in candlelight,
floating, then
vanishing into the night.

She slumped in her chair,
speech slurred,
and ordered me to clean
the purple stain
from her dress,
from the splintered floor,
from my memory.

FRANK LAPENA

Left: *Spring Spirit,* 1987, acrylic on canvas, 48 x 36 inches.
Photo by Mike Hills. Right: *Blue Shadow Spirit,* 1991, acrylic
on canvas, 40 x 30 inches. Photo courtesy of the artist.

POEMS BY SHAUNNA OTEKA MCCOVEY

I STILL EAT ALL OF MY MEALS WITH A MUSSEL SHELL

Creation stories
thespiritbeings
have long been disputed
emergedfrom
by theories of
theground
evolution and
atKenek
strait crossings.

Because our rivers
halfbreedshave
were once filled
agodthatis
with gold
neitherIndian
our women were violated
orwhite
in the worst imaginable way.

Only a few
prayersgo
still know
unheardwhen
the formula that
notspokenin
will bring the salmon
ournativetongues
up the river.

If you cannot see
Istilleat
between the lines
allofmymeals
then your collected facts
witha
will never constitute
musselshell
knowledge.

CAPITALISTS?

Forty-five bucks
and a good sweat later
the Shaman who said
he was from

a long line of
Cherokee holy men
sang one last
Lakota song,

gave you a
Seminole medicine pouch
and a Kiowa name,
told you that you'd

now received an
Indian education,
a new spirituality,
and to, next time,

take advantage of his
"Friends Drum Free" coupon.

JAMES LUNA
High-Tech Peace Pipe (detail), 2000,
performance/installation. Photo by William Gullette.

THE BRUSH DANCE BOY LIVES IN PHOENIX, ARIZONA

SHAUNNA OTEKA MCCOVEY

For Louisa McConnell

Sing me songs
of smoke and root,
in full regalia, abalone swaying.
Pull your arrows from
a quiver made of me.

Tonight I went outside
and for the first time
since I've been in this
place far from home
the stars shone brighter
than the city lights,
the Earth stopped, still,
for just one moment and I saw
the Brush Dance Boy
dancing in the full moon,
watching over me
like he has always done.

Sing me dreams
of smoke and root,
feel the sun rise in my heart
after the morning dance.
Jump center into my soul.

FRANK TUTTLE

Flags and Whispers (detail), 1992, mixed media on wood,
36 x 42 inches. Photo courtesy of Frank LaPena.

POEMS BY SHAUNNA OTEKA MCCOVEY

TEMPO OF LOVE

Presto,
it was like fire
consuming everything in its path,
starving flames that would not die
or let you breathe.

(She sang an Indian love song,)

Allegro,
it moved as though
fueled by something unknown,
something without control,
so you conceded.

(and the song floated like a dream,)

Andante,
then it rested inside,
came to a quiet, comfortable place,
a stow-away in your eyes
wanting to give pieces at a time.

(made its way through different houses,)

Adagio,
it let you catch your breath,
step away and find yourself,
what you had lost in the remnants of smoke,
and in the slowing, it grew from the ash.

(and found a home where it now sleeps).

THE ROOT

For my sister, Julia

I'll weave
with good intention

the story of our lives,
my heart speaks,

without invention,
of how I know

where we belong,
in our place of

Snake's Nose and Swallow's Tail,
of bleached beargrass

and maidenhair,
of love designed

by our own hands,
held so resolutely

by the root that is you.

DUGAN AGUILAR

This page: *Lucy Lowry,* 2000, b&w photograph, 7½ x 9½
inches. Facing page: *Tuolumne MeWuk Rancheria
Roundhouse,* 1993, b&w photograph, 6 x 9 inches.

FRITZ SCHOLDER

Left: *Indian Land #2*, 1980, acrylic on canvas, 80 x 68 inches.
Above: *Indian Contemplating Columbus*, 1992, lithograph,
59¾ x 40¼ inches. Photos by Bill McLemore.

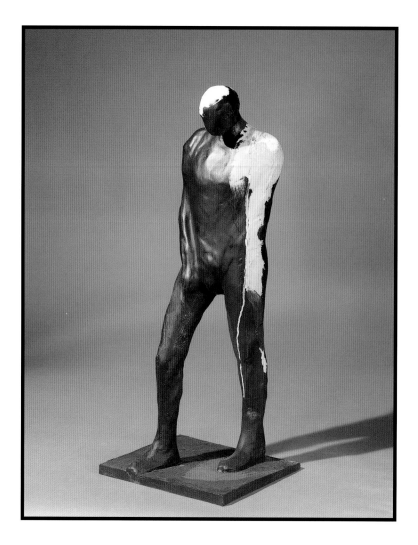

FRITZ SCHOLDER

Above: *Painted Man #1*, 1991, bronze (edition 1/2),
27 inches tall. Right: *Dakota & Felix*, 1993, mixed media
collage, 11 x 15 inches. Photos by Bill McLemore.

WHEN MY GREAT-GREAT-GRANDFATHER TOM SMITH CAUSED THE 1906 EARTHQUAKE

GREG SARRIS

His sister was there, the one who covered her head with the lace mantilla Captain Smith had given their mother; yes, and she had a child with her, the niece with doubting eyes who at ten could read and write. And Big Jose brought along two light-skinned sisters from the Haupt ranch, each of them fine-looking women who certainly had placed their bets on Big Jose. But he would show the pretty women, he'd show his sister and the doubting child, he'd show everyone in the world that this time he would win once and for all.

Their battles were famous. Shows of power, people called them. At the Haupt ranch, over in Freestone, up and down the coast. Like this: "I can roll a big rock across camp," Big Jose said, and a boulder the size of a fifty-gallon drum rolled from one end of the camp to another. "Four raccoons will come here walking on their hind legs," he countered, and not only did the raccoons enter the camp upright but also backwards. "Well, then, I'll make it rain," Big Jose said. "Then I'll make it thunder," he countered again. On and on it went.

This time the onlookers gathered behind a livery stable just above the bay—Bodega Bay. That's what people who tell the story say. And it was early morning before he stood up and pronounced himself ready. No songs, no dance. He faced the east, where there was light, and only said, "Answer me."

At first nothing, a few sparks lifting from the campfire. Then more sparks; sparks and more sparks and that's when they felt the earth shaking from below the fire, radiating from the center of the flames, stronger and stronger, shaking and rolling, the world tipping this way and that, on and on so that by the time it stopped the livery stable was an enormous torch lighting the hills and bay for miles; yes, lighting the hills and bay and pelting them with the hysterical whinnies of burning horses.

His sister's lace mantilla fell to the ground. The little girl's eyes widened and held the fire. The pretty sisters hiked their dresses to their thighs and ran off. Someone shouted. "Enough, you won." But he didn't see or hear these things. He ran off too, deeper and deeper into the hills with clouds of black smoke following him like ghosts.

KATHLEEN SMITH
To-To Dancer, Coastal Style, watercolor, 24 x 15 inches.
Photo by Beverly R. Ortiz.

KATHLEEN SMITH

My People's Home, Upper Dry Creek, watercolor,
30 x 22 inches. Photo by Beverly R. Ortiz.

LITERARY LUNCHEON: IOWA CITY

According to the windows
that face the slow-spilling brown river
we are sipping not our coffee
but blizzard winds that surprise us
rolling from the north.
Still-bare trees
are slowly colored white
and the earth implies
this
is the source
of the cold I feel.
Not so.
The great ones gather
at the university buffet
like cattle around
alfalfa and barley.
I maintain
without willing it
an Indian invisibility.

FORTY, TREMBLING

She bore no children
but ghosts emerged
from between her legs.

Dare to believe
that roots can be built
like a pot
in ascending circles
and that skin
will just naturally form
copper sheets
on the bones.
Promise
that a name will appear
blazing from the cliff,
that this is a harvest
large enough for life
and her life is not
half empty but has much
farther to go.
Step Softly.
She is not of this world
and no one rides
to the rescue.

(Coarsegold, 1992)

DETECTIVE WORK

Found the songs first
in little pieces
under a stone. Took all my strength
to gently roll the stone
and prod them out

but behind the yellow piss-pine
crouched the trickster, waiting
to put a mountain there.

GERALD CLARKE

Cahuilla Sounds, Cahuilla Lives, 1997, baseball bat and
painted gourd with audio, 10 x 38 x 10 inches.
Photo courtesy of the artist.

IS IT CRAZY TO WANT TO UNRAVEL

like a dandelion gone to seed,
leaving nothing behind but a dent
or not even that to touch or burn
or remember. This is the way
winter begins—
    with the angry moth
    who grips the window screen
    and freezes into an opal.
    Well, that's one way to go—
    just get harder. Or I could dissolve
    as disobedient women do in the Bible
    their solemn salt hands still pointing
    to the pleasures of sin.
    I could evaporate or liquefy
    or become dust or turn sideways
    before a funhouse mirror
    to become a needle
    becoming nothing.

I could scream so mightily
that only sound could survive.
I could cry myself dry,
be sifted by the desert wind
that burns my summer gold hills.
Or I could fly apart
    and watch my whirling blood
    form galaxies in the air,
    spatter on the men
    who hammer to death
    the trees and remark
    that a women just
    was standing there
and now
poof she is gone.

(Coursegold, 1991)

HOLODECK

WENDY ROSE

(with apologies to "Star Trek: The Next Generation")

When they come
I go into my head
private holodeck
so easy
    like breathing
and when that room is locked
and I am trapped in the world
it is like when
    the breathing stops.

        Program: ongoing saga
        of voices
        that beg me not to die
        when I am lost
        to forces so great
        so out of control
        it is not just loss
        but tribunal,
        a thing to be worn
        like armband or badge
        so that every face and hand
        stops, knows and agrees, remembers
        there is reason to grieve.
        Baskets full of regret
        but no one scolds me
        for feeling sorry for myself again.
        I ask everyone to sit and listen.
        The miracle is that they do.

MIKE RODRIGUEZ

Untitled, 2001, copper etching, 4¾ x 5¼ inches.
Photo courtesy of the artist.

PARRIS BUTLER
five red streaks, 1996, monoprint, 6 x 4 inches.
Photo courtesy of the artist.

GRASS VALLEY

STEPHEN MEADOWS

The dirt is red here
stone speckles the ground
a light snow has fallen
in the night
the room smells of matches
her husband is dying
she splits up the wood
in her bathrobe
morning by morning
releasing the days

POEMS BY STEPHEN MEADOWS

JOHN'S SONG

At the end of the counter
the old man's falsetto quavers
brittle as his cup
some tune from the twenties
his voice a frayed reed
or the sound of bees
nesting wood
It is his last October
Wrists about to let his hands
go the way of fruit
he does not lay them down
though they shake ever slightly
out of the sleeves
It is a song from the twenties
he moves as he sings
the way I've seen sick gulls
rocking in the wind
he does not care who watches
the white dusted fragment
of his body and the frail song mythic
and fragile as his sight

AT THE CROSSING

A chainsaw dismembers the silence
of a white afternoon

in a pasture
the crackle of fires
in pruned orchard wood

little to do midwinter
but cut and burn trash

drink warm booze
in long sleeves

and watch the smoke
crossing the river
enter in among the trees

THE DOE

Cresting the ridge
at dawn
in the dark
the engine of the
forty six pickup
the lights
on the road
she dives out of the brush
in my headlights
is blind
quivering in the dust
she cannot believe
her death
as men with knives
lead her into the trees

NORRIS RANCH

Red and yellow leaves
share afternoon light
each shade upon another
creating honey out of air
Flies are haphazard
their buzzing and the groan
of an icebox intermit
with calls from a small child
refusing to sleep
The sun in November just
an hour above the sea
watched over this ridge
through redwood and madrone
A ragged day passes
beyond the reach
of this poem
coming apart as the weblines
of a spider drift in
and out of view

REWEAVING THE WORLD OHLONE

STEPHEN MEADOWS

For Linda Yamane

Enmeshing
with bone awl
with curved tooth
with dreaming
Again living patience
the slow walk
and choosing
The arms
and the fingers
of plants
the bent branches
the willow
the cattail
the root
the crisp grasses
The green limb
the gold stem
the soft flesh
the cleansing
the sheer thought
the taut hand
the earth's
whirling music
In your palm
in your lap
in your sphere
in your circle
This basket
this dance
upon the ground

LINDA YAMANE

Abover: *Coiled Basket*, 1999, sedge, willow, and bulrush with glass beads, 10¼ x 2¼ inches. Photo by Dugan Aguilar. Right, top: *Necklace of Abalone and Clamshell Beads* (detail), 1995, clamshell beads, abalone pendants, buckskin tie, 16 inches long. Right, bottom: *Coiled Feather Basket*, 1997, willow foundation wrapped with sedge, red-wing blackbird and mallard duck feathers, and olivella disk beads, 3 inches wide. Photos by Linda Yamane.

CONTRIBUTOR BIOGRAPHIES

DUGAN AGUILAR (Paiute/Pit River/Maidu) works as a graphic artist in the advertising department of the *Sacramento Bee*. The first college graduate in his family, he received a degree in industrial technology and design from California State University, Fresno, and subsequently took photography classes at the University of Nevada, Reno. He is inspired by the work of Ansel Adams and the basketweavers who "give" him pictures.

LINDA AGUILAR (Chumash) graduated from the University of California, Santa Barbara, with a degree in art. She is a prolific and playful basketweaver, best known for her tightly coiled horsehair baskets decorated with shells, beads, and other material she "picks up and stores in her pockets." Her work has been presented to Nelson Mandela and the Dalai Lama, and one of her baskets is in the collection of the Smithsonian Institution's Renwick Gallery.

RICK BARTOW (Yurok) received a B.A. in art education from Western Oregon State College before serving in the Vietnam War. His pastel drawings, prints, and sculptures have been exhibited throughout the world. Of his ever-evolving technique he writes, "Using Coyote's tail for a brush and Raven's beak to make my marks, I am blind to my destination." He is exclusively represented by the Froelick Gallery in Portland.

GEORGE BLAKE (Hupa/Yurok) is a versatile carver whose repertoire includes traditional objects, such as elk-antler spoons and dugout canoes, as well as contemporary sculptural works in clay, wood, and antler. He studied art at the University of California, Davis, and has served as

director of the Hoopa Tribal Museum. In 1991 he received the National Endowment for the Arts Heritage Award for his efforts to preserve traditional California Indian arts. He lives on the Hoopa Valley Indian Reservation.

PARRIS BUTLER (Mohave/Cherokee) explores tribal designs in a range of Western media, producing works in a style he calls "figurative geometric abstraction." He studied creative writing and two-dimensional arts at the Institute of American Indian Arts in Santa Fe, where he quickly became disenchanted with the "rampant commercialism of Southwest art and culture." He now lives and works in Oakland. He finds inspiration in "the physical environment and in the events of the contemporary world" and strives to communicate the "essential form" of his subjects.

LORENCITA CARPENTER (Hupa) was born and raised in the Hoopa Valley. She studied photography and other contemporary studio arts at Humboldt State University. In addition to taking photographs, she paints, makes jewelry, and writes poetry.

GERALD CLARKE (Cahuilla) was born in Hemet and raised in southern California. He studied art at universities in Arkansas and Texas and earned his M.F.A. from Stephen F. Austin State University. He now lives in Ada, Oklahoma, where he teaches art at East Central University. In 1997, he was selected to participate in the Heard Museum's Seventh Native American Fine Art Invitational.

HARRY FONSECA (Nisenan Maidu) was born and raised in California and educated at Sacramento City College and California State University, Sacramento. He currently resides in Santa Fe. Over the years his paintings have addressed a myriad of topics, including the California Gold Rush, rock art, the Maidu creation myth, and the California missions. His work has been exhibited throughout the world.

JANICE GOULD (Konkow Maidu) grew up in Berkeley and graduated magna cum laude from the University of California, Berkeley, where she received degrees in linguistics (B.A.) and English (M.A.). She earned her Ph.D. at the University of New Mexico with a dissertation on the poetry of Muscogee writer Joy Harjo. Her poems have been published in numerous journals and anthologies and collected in two books: *Beneath My Heart* (Firebrand Press, 1990) and *Earthquake Weather* (University of Arizona Press, 1996). She currently plays guitar and teaches poetry and English in Portland.

JEAN LAMARR (Paiute/Pit River) is a printmaker, papermaker, muralist, and installation artist whose work frequently depicts such issues as the status of women, land, and tribal sovereignty. She lives in Susanville, where she is the owner and director of the Native American Graphic Workshop. She attended the University of California, Berkeley.

FRANK LAPENA (Nomtipom Wintu) is an internationally exhibited painter and published poet. His family and the ceremonial events of his tribe inspire his work. "Like life," he has written, "art is not always pretty or easy." He is professor emeritus of art and ethnic studies at California State University, Sacramento, and a member of the Maidu Dancers and Traditionalists. He frequently writes about the arts for *News from Native California*.

JUDITH LOWRY (Mountain Maidu/Hamawi Pit River) entered and won her first art contest in Germany, at the age of six, and has been making art ever since. While her first training was in photography, most of her subsequent works have been large-scale acrylic paintings with figurative or narrative content. She is inspired by the early Renaissance as much as by the storytelling traditions of Native Californians. In 2001 she was one of twenty artists nationwide to receive the annual Joan Mitchell Foundation Award.

JAMES LUNA (Luiseño) works as an academic counselor at Palomar College, near his home on the La Jolla Indian Reservation. He has performed at universities, art galleries, and museums across the United States and Canada. His installations have been described as "transforming gallery spaces into battlefields" where the audience is confronted with the nature of cultural identity and the dangers of cultural misinterpretation.

L. FRANK MANRIQUEZ (Tongva/Acjachmem) is known for her backwards handwriting and coyote cartoons, which are collected in *Acorn Soup* (Heyday Books, 1999). In addition to painting and drawing, she also works in soapstone and other traditional materials. She is a board member of the California Indian Basketweavers Association and a frequent contributor to *News from Native California*.

BRADLEY MARSHALL (Hupa) is a regalia-maker for the Hoopa, Karuk, and Yurok tribes. He is also versed in the art of carving wood and elk antler. He started making

regalia when, after spending nearly a decade in San Francisco, away from his homeland, he woke up from a dream speaking his language. He currently serves on the Clarke Museum's board of directors and works for the Environmental Protection Agency.

SHAUNNA OTEKA MCCOVEY (Yurok/Karuk) started writing poetry at the age of six, while growing up on the Yurok reservation in northern California. She holds a master's degree in social work from Arizona State University and is currently studying environmental law at Vermont Law School.

STEPHEN MEADOWS (Ohlone) holds degrees from the University of California, Santa Cruz, and San Francisco State University. He has been influenced and inspired by the poems of ancient China as well as the work of Dylan Thomas, Kenneth Rexroth, Gary Snyder, and the Beat poets of San Francisco.

DEBORAH MIRANDA (Esselen) received her Ph.D. from the University of Washington and is currently assistant professor of English at Pacific Lutheran University. Before finishing her degree, she worked as a berry-picker, a teacher of special-needs children, and a housecleaner. Her book of poems, *Indian Cartography* (Greenfield Review Press, 1999), won the North American Native Authors First Book Award.

LINDA NOEL (Konkow Maidu) has been described as a "twenty-first-century salmon in disguise." She works for a tribal vocational rehabilitation program and resides in Mendocino County. Her poems have been published by Pot Shards Press and *News from Native California*.

MIKE RODRIGUEZ (Luiseño) is best known for colorful, large-scale public artworks, including murals and graffiti on display in Sacramento. While he still participates in public art projects, he has moved into prints and other smaller-scale works that explore the power of line and composition. All his works employ a gritty, industrial style that evokes the harsh reality of tribal survival and urban life.

WENDY ROSE (Miwok/Hopi) was born and raised in Oakland. Her poems have been published in numerous books, including *Lost Copper* (Malki Museum Press, 1980) and *Bone Dance: New and Selected Poems, 1965–1993* (University of Arizona Press, 1994). She currently teaches at Fresno City College, where she is also coordinator of American Indian Studies.

SYLVIA ROSS (Chukchansi) was born and raised in Los Angeles, apart from her family's culture. After graduating from high school, she painted cels for Walt Disney Productions. Once married, she returned to school and earned a B.A. from Fresno State College. She then moved with her family to Porterville, where she taught school on the Tule River Indian Reservation. Now retired, she writes poetry, draws, and researches her family heritage.

GREG SARRIS (Coast Miwok) is the author of several books, including *Grand Avenue* (Hyperion, 1994), a collection of short stories, and the novel *Watermelon Nights* (Hyperion, 1998). He received his Ph.D. in Modern Thought and Literature from Stanford University. He is currently serving his fifth elected term as chairman of his tribe, the Federated Indians of the Graton Rancheria, formerly known as the Federated Coast Miwok. He teaches at Loyola Marymount University.

FRITZ SCHOLDER (Luiseño) is considered one of the founders of the contemporary Native American fine art

movement. He studied with Wayne Thiebaud at Sacramento City College, earned his Master of Fine Arts degree at the University of Arizona, and taught painting at the Institute of American Indian Arts before retiring to devote all his time to artwork. He currently lives in Scottsdale, Arizona.

KATHLEEN SMITH (Bodega Miwok/Dry Creek Pomo) grew up in the Healdsburg area, the seventh of nine children. She aspired to be an artist from early childhood and graduated from the San Francisco Art Institute in 1977. Over the years she has held such diverse jobs as park naturalist, art instructor, archaeology field technician, and foods columnist for *News from Native California*.

RICHARD STEWART (Owens Valley Paiute) is a storyteller, basketweaver, ceramicist, printmaker, and poet. He lectures extensively on the Manzanar War Relocation Center and the ethnography and archaeology of the Owens Valley Paiutes. In describing his mysterious connection to Japan, he writes: "I am Japanese/Paiute, Hoichi the Earless, a blind musician singing the epic poem of removal and relocation for an audience I cannot see."

BRIAN TRIPP (Karuk) served in Vietnam before attending Humboldt State University, where he majored in art. His paintings and sculptures incorporate eclectic found objects, such as tin foil, sticks, and bicycle reflectors, as well as traditional symbols from northern California basketry. Like many of his peers in this collection, he participates in the ceremonies of his tribe as a dancer and singer.

FRANK TUTTLE (Yuki/Wailaki/Konkow Maidu) holds a degree in art from Humboldt State University. When not painting, he serves as director of community outreach for the Consolidated Tribal Health Project in Redwood Valley.

DARRYL WILSON (Achumawe/Atsugewi) was born in 1939 at the confluence of the Fall and Pit Rivers in northeastern California. He holds a B.A. from the University of California, Davis, and a Ph.D. from the University of Arizona. His autobiography, *The Morning the Sun Went Down*, was published in 1998 by Heyday Books.

LINDA YAMANE (Rumsien Ohlone) is a basketweaver, storyteller, and writer. She was a member of the founding board of directors of the California Indian Basketweavers Association and has been active in reviving Rumsien language and traditions. She is the author of two children's books, *When the World Ended, How Hummingbird Got Fire, How People Were Made* (Oyate, 1995) and *The Snake That Lived in the Santa Cruz Mountains & Other Ohlone Stories* (Oyate, 1998), and is currently writing a history of Monterey's Indian community from the time of European contact to the mid-twentieth century.

This project is funded in part by The San Francisco Foundation, the community foundation of the Bay Area, and by the California Arts Council, a state agency. Any findings, opinions, or conclusions contained therein are not necessarily those of the California Arts Council.